The Missions of California

WITHDRAWN

Mission San José

Amy Margaret

The Rosen Publishing Group's
PowerKids Press™
New York

To Dionne and Derek, California kids I love so much.

Published in 2000, 2003 by The Rosen Publishing Group, Inc.
29 East 21st Street, New York, NY 10010

Revised Edition 2003

Book Design: Danielle Primiceri

Photo Credits: pp. 1, 4, 20, 21, 30, 31, 33, 37, 42, 43, 44, 45, 46, 47, 48, 49, 50, 51 © Cristina Taccone; pp. 13, 32 © Michael Ward; p. 6A © SuperStock; p. 6B Courtesy of National Park Service, Cabrillo National Monument; p. 7 c/o The Rosen Publishing Group circa 1800s; pp. 11, 28 © The Granger Collection, New York; pp. 12, 27 © Department of Special Collections, University of Southern California Library; pp. 14 © North Wind Picture Archive; p. 17 © Baldwin H. Ward/CORBIS-Bettmann; pp. 22, 24 © The Bancroft Library; p. 23, 29, 40 © CORBIS-Bettmann; p. 35 © Archive Photos; p. 36 by Tim Hall; p. 39 © Albin Greger; pp. 52, 57 © Christine Innamorato.

Editorial Consultant Coordinator: Karen Fontanetta, M.A., Curator, Mission San Miguel Arcángel
Historical Photo Consultants: Thomas L. Davis, M. Div., M.A.
                              Michael K. Ward, M.A.

Margaret, Amy.
    Mission San José / by Amy Margaret. — 1st ed.
        p. cm. — (The missions of California)
    Includes bibliographical references and index.
    Summary: Discusses the founding, building, operation, closing, and restoration of the San José Mission and its role in California history.
    ISBN 0-8239-5897-3 (lib. bdg.)
    1. Mission San José (Alameda County, Calif.)—History Juvenile literature. 2. Spanish mission buildings—California—Alameda County—History Juvenile literature. 3. Franciscans—California—Alameda County—History Juvenile literature. 4. Ohlone Indians—Missions—California—Alameda County—History Juvenile literature. 5. California—History—To 1846 Juvenile literature. [1. Mission San José (Alameda County, Calif.)—History. 2. Missions—California. 3. Indians of North America—California—Missions. 4. California—History—To 1846.] I. Title. II. Series.
F869.M66M37 1999
979.4'65—dc21
                                                            99-24610
                                                              CIP

Manufactured in the United States of America

Contents

Spain Explores America

Mission San José was the 14th of the 21 missions to be built along the California coast. It was founded in 1797, by a Spanish friar named Fray Fermín Francisco Lasuén. The word *fray* means friar in Spanish. Mission San José flourished until 1832. It was one of the most prosperous missions on the northern coast. The mission system was started by rulers in Spain who wanted to colonize foreign lands. They thought the system would be an effective way to develop the rich land of California.

Although hundreds of American Indian tribes had made their homes in the California area for thousands of years, the Spanish thought these people were "uncivilized." The American Indians didn't share the same religion, nor did they work, play, or even eat in ways similar to the Europeans. Today we can appreciate the differences of various cultures around the world, but in the eighteenth century the Spaniards thought they could help the Indians by making them more like the Europeans.

As the 21 missions were built from 1769 to 1823, the Spanish tried to teach the California Indians to live and act like the Europeans. The missionaries' main goal was to convert the local California Indians to Christianity. The Spanish king and church leaders believed it was their duty to convert and protect the Indians, but also to claim the land. The attempt to change the way these people lived eventually led to the destruction of the lifestyle the California Indians had led for centuries.

The Age of Exploration

When the rulers of Spain sent out their explorers in the 1400s and 1500s, they were not looking for people to become Spanish citizens.

◀ *Mission San José church and cemetery as it stands today.*

5

Rather, the Spanish were eager to find treasures and new land to claim as their own.

Christopher Columbus, an Italian explorer sailing for Spain, discovered the so-called New World, or North America, South America, and Central America, for Spain. He was followed by several other brave men, including Ferdinand Magellan, Juan Rodríguez Cabrillo, and Sebastián Vizcaíno.

▲
Famous explorer Christopher Columbus

Juan Rodríguez Cabrillo

Juan Rodríguez Cabrillo was a Portuguese sailor who sailed for Spain. He and his crew were probably the first explorers to sail past the land that would one day be the foundation for Mission San José. In 1542, Cabrillo left port in New Spain, the area that is now Mexico, to find a water route that would connect the Pacific Ocean and Atlantic Ocean. He never found it, but he sailed from the area that is today San Diego Bay in southern California all the way up to what is now the state of Oregon. Though Cabrillo died on this remarkable journey, he is known as one of the first Spanish explorers of California.

Cabrillo claimed the land of California as Spanish territory. This was the last territory on the borders of New Spain.

▲
Spanish explorer Juan Rodríguez Cabrillo

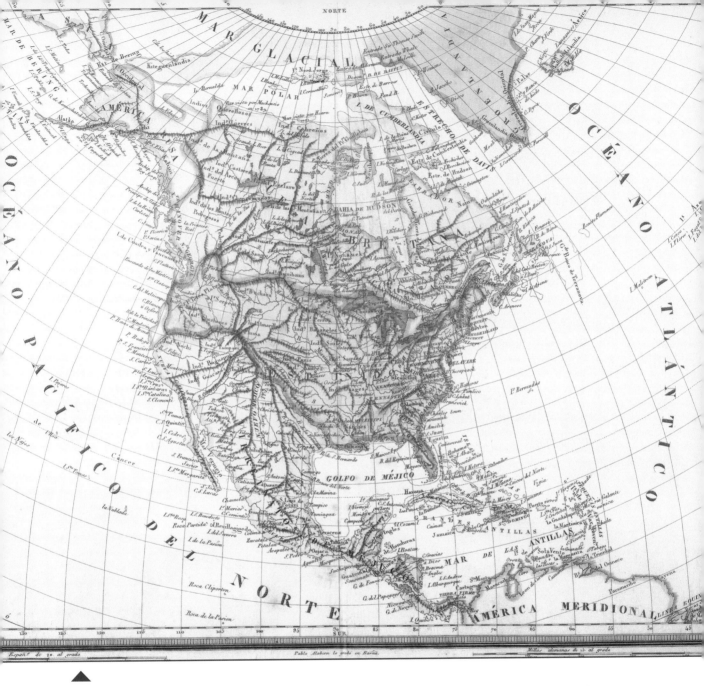

This map of the New World is from around 1800. California and the American West were still part of New Spain at this time.

7

At the time, California consisted of what is now the state of California and the Baja Peninsula of Mexico. It was divided into two parts, Alta, or upper, California and Baja, or lower, California.

Sebastián Vizcaíno

Sixty years later, in 1602, Spanish explorer Sebastián Vizcaíno made the same journey as Cabrillo. His goal, like Cabrillo's, was to find a waterway connecting the Pacific and Atlantic Oceans. As Vizcaíno made his way up from Baja California to Alta California, he met several groups of California Indians.

Vizcaíno was as unsuccessful as Cabrillo in finding a water route so the viceroy of New Spain decided to stop funding journeys to Alta California. No Spanish ships sailed into the area for 160 years. Then in the 1760s, Spanish rulers sent their soldiers and explorers back into Alta California when they found out that Russian and English ships had been spotted along the shores there.

Spain wanted to keep the land Cabrillo and Vizcaíno had claimed. This time, though, the Spanish wouldn't just send a couple of ships to claim the land for their own. They planned to settle the land and to turn the California Indians living there into Spanish citizens.

This map shows the areas of Alta California and Baja California. ▶

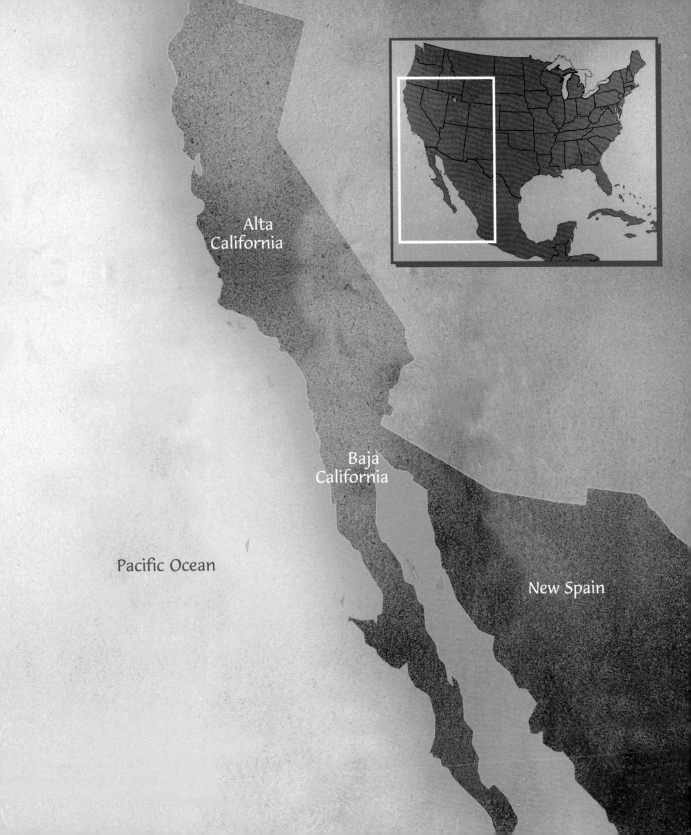

Alta
California

Baja
California

New Spain

Pacific Ocean

The California Indians

The Ohlone Indians

The Ohlone people were one of the main groups of Indians to make their home in Alta California. Of course the Ohlone lived there long before there was a San Francisco, a state of California, or even a land called America.

Many groups of Ohlone lived all along the northern coast of Alta California. They spoke different languages and dialects but had no written language. For food, the Ohlone hunted deer, antelope, ducks, and geese. The Pacific Ocean was a rich source of seafood.

Out of all the natural resources the Ohlone used, such as berries and mushrooms, they depended mostly on acorns. The Indians used all the different acorns growing in the area. They ground the acorns into flour for bread and porridge. The California Indian tribes did not plant their own food.

The Ohlone Way of Life

The Ohlone lived in villages numbering from 50 to several hundred members. Every village had an assembly house and a sweathouse. Constructed from tule, or tightly woven reeds, the assembly house was used for large gatherings and could hold the entire village population. Individual homes were also made of tule. When a home was infested with bugs, or became dirty over time, its occupants burned it down and built another in its place. The sweathouse was a small hut where Indians cleansed their bodies through sweating. They went through this ritual for a variety of reasons, such as curing an illness, healing a skin disease, or preparing for a hunt.

Many California Indians often danced and sang in their traditional ceremonies. ▶

The Indians used sweathouses to cleanse their bodies and their spirits.

Every village was led by a chief, one of the wealthiest members of the tribe. He or she shared the wealth with everyone who needed it. It was the chief's responsibility to make sure that visitors were given food and a place to stay.

The shaman was the other leader of the tribe. The shaman could be male or female and took care of all religious matters. The tribe believed that the shaman was able to control the weather and heal sick people.

Ohlone tribes looked after their members with care. Children were not just raised by their mothers and fathers, but by their extended families as well. The older tribespeople were treated with great respect and the younger members listened to them carefully. Days in the village were usually spent gathering, hunting, and preparing food. Children and adults had plenty of time to play.

The men were skilled hunters, and they took pride in their handmade bows and arrows. All weapons and tools were made from wood, rocks, or animal bones. The women made baskets, which they used to separate seeds from plants, carry and store water, cook food, or carry almost any load.

Not much of a day-to-day schedule was needed for Ohlone Indians. They did what they needed to survive, and they spent their free time enjoying nature. Their generous and hard-working attitudes probably made it easy for the Spanish missionaries to enter their lives in the late 1700s. As the Ohlone moved into missions such as Mission San José, their lives changed forever.

▲

The Ohlone Indians were great hunters and fishermen.

13

The California Mission System

By the time Mission San José was founded in 1797, 13 other missions had already been built. Under the guidance of Spanish missionaries, or friars, the missions were on their way to becoming thriving communities.

The purpose of the missions was to bring local California Indians to a central location and make them Christians, and later, Spanish citizens. When Indians converted, they were baptized, or immersed in water as a symbol of their belief in the Christian god. They were then considered neophytes, or new converts. The neophytes, under the missionaries' supervision, worked at tasks around the missions, such as cattle raising, farming, and blanket weaving.

Each mission developed an economy, so that people who were a part of the mission system were self-sufficient. As more people came to live and work at a mission, its economy got stronger, enabling growth. The Spanish thought that after 10 years the missions could be secularized, or turned from religious institutions into civic ones.

The goal of the Spanish missionaries was for the California Indians to be tax-paying Spanish citizens at the time of secularization. The missionaries thought that once the Indians had learned the Christian way of life and worship, their native lands could be returned to them. This did not happen as the missionaries planned. Many missionaries thought the Indians weren't ready for secularization after 10 years. The Indians never got their land back.

◀ *Mission San José as it appeared in the 1850s*

The Founders of the California Missions

Fray Junípero Serra

Fray Junípero Serra was born Miguel José Serra in Majorca, Spain, in 1713. From the time he was a child, his parents encouraged his interest in the church. When he was old enough, they sent him to a school run by Franciscans, an order of priests founded by Saint Francis of Assisi in the thirteenth century. They had to live by strict guidelines, including never marrying, taking a vow of poverty, and always acting in complete obedience to God.

In 1737, Fray Serra became a Franciscan friar and changed his first name in honor of a favored priest as was the tradition of the Franciscans. Miguel José chose Junípero, a companion of Saint Francis whom Serra greatly admired.

After Fray Junípero Serra graduated from the Convento de San Francisco de Palma as an ordained Catholic priest, he worked in Spain for about 12 years, excelling at any task he was given. While in Spain, he taught many students who were as passionate about the ministry as he was.

In 1749, Fray Serra, along with Fray Francisco Palóu, a former pupil, and Fray Juan Crespí, a missionary and explorer, sailed across the Atlantic Ocean to New Spain to do missionary work with the Indians living in the New World. They had heard of the Indians who lived so differently from the way the Europeans did. Fray Serra and his companions were excited about sharing their message of Christianity with the Indians.

Frays Serra, Palóu, and Crespí sailed to Veracruz, New Spain, but their

This is a statue of Fray Junípero Serra with Juan Evangilista. ▶
Serra always dreamed of doing missionary work.

station was in Mexico City, New Spain, 269 miles (433 km) away. Serra and another friar decided to walk to Mexico City. He and his companion shuffled along the dusty dirt trails, the hot sun penetrating their woolen robes. Nothing, though, could discourage Fray Serra and his companion. As long as Fray Serra could remember, he had wanted to be a missionary. Finally he had the opportunity.

When they arrived in Mexico City, Fray Serra worked as a priest for the College of San Fernando for 17 years. In 1767, the Spanish rulers needed someone to supervise the missions in Baja California. Fray Serra was chosen as mission president.

Alta California

After working in Baja California for a year, Fray Serra was chosen to establish a mission system all along the coast of Alta California. As

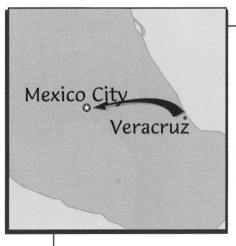

On the long trip from Veracruz to Mexico City, Fray Serra was bitten on the left foot by an insect. His leg became infected and almost prevented him from completing the journey. After a rest, the two continued on under Fray Serra's command. This wound continued to bother Fray Serra for the rest of his life, but it rarely kept him from visiting new sites and founding more missions.

the president, he was to oversee the friars at each mission and find new sites for future missions.

One of Serra's first jobs was to accompany Captain Gaspár de Portolá on a land expedition of Alta California in March 1769. In July, only four months after they left Baja California, Fray Serra founded the first California mission, Mission San Diego de Alcalá. This was the first permanent European settlement in California.

Fray Junípero Serra is known as the father of the California missions. He founded the first nine missions and developed the plan to establish California missions from the southern point of California up to the San Francisco Bay. Each mission was built along a road called El Camino Real, meaning "The Royal Road," so visitors could travel along the coast and have places to stay.

○ San Francisco Solano
○ San Rafael Arcángel
○ San Francisco de Asís
○ San José

○ Santa Clara de Asís
○ Santa Cruz
○ San Juan Bautista
○ San Carlos Borromeo de Carmelo
○ Nuestra Señora de la Soledad

○ San Antonio de Padua
○ San Miguel Arcángel

○ San Luis Obispo de Tolosa

○ La Purísima Concepción
○ Santa Inés
○ Santa Bárbara
○ San Buenaventura

○ San Fernando Rey de España
○ San Gabriel Arcángel

○ San Juan Capistrano

○ San Luis Rey de Francia

○ San Diego de Alcalá

Fray Fermín Francisco Lasuén

Fray Serra died in 1784. A year later, Fray Fermín Lasuén replaced Fray Serra as the leader of the missions. Lasuén had also been born in Spain and had made the journey to New Spain in 1759. When the California missions were first started, Lasuén had already worked at some of them. Under Lasuén's leadership as mission president, nine more missions were founded, including Mission San José.

During Fray Lasuén's career as mission president from 1785 until his death in 1803, he doubled the number of California missions. He was buried next to his friend Fray Serra at Mission San Carlos Borromeo, in Carmel. This stone marks Fray Lasuén's burial place at Mission San Carlos Borromeo.

▲

The bell on the right side of the photo marks El Camino Real, the road that links each mission on the coast of California.

Founding and Building
Mission San José

On the warm summer day of June 11, 1797, the 14th California mission, San José, was founded. This was 13 years after the death of Fray Serra, but his memory lived on as the missions continued to be built along Alta California's coast. Fray Fermín Lasuén, Serra's successor, founded the San José mission, named after Saint Joseph, the husband of Jesus' mother, Mary.

▲

Mission San José was named after Saint Joseph.

Within 48 hours of the founding service, shelters were quickly constructed. Converted Indians from nearby Mission Santa Clara de Asís helped build the shelters. Mission Santa Clara de Asís and Mission San Francisco de Asís sent supplies and livestock to help Mission San José get started.

In its first year, only 33 Ohlone Indians joined the mission. More Indians started joining when the friars offered each Indian new clothes, blankets, and food. The Indians were baptized into Christianity when the friars thought they were ready.

The neophytes were told that they must live at the mission, only occasionally being allowed to visit their old villages. The Spanish missionaries thought they were helping the California Indians by keeping them from their old way of life. Some Indians did not like this rule, or any of the rules that were imposed on them at the mission.

◄ *Mission San José was the fourteenth California mission founded by the Franciscan friars.*

23

When both Fray Serra and Fray Lasuén were looking for new sites on which to build missions, they had several things to consider. The land needed to have fertile soil for growing crops and plenty of fresh water. Most of all, the land needed to be near large groups of California Indians in order to convert them to Christianity.

Building the Mission

When the friars set out to build a mission, they first constructed the church. The other buildings were set up around the church, forming an open area in the middle, called a quadrangle. The church was a simple building with only three windows. The ceiling was 24 feet (7.3 m) high and the walls were 4 feet (1.2 m) thick. The missionaries later decided to shorten the bell tower to the height of the church loft instead of above the church's roof, as it stood at many other missions. San José's permanent church was completed in 1809.

By 1810, 60 *rancherías*, or houses for the neophytes, had been built. As the mission population grew over the next 15 years, new *rancherías* were added to the mission.

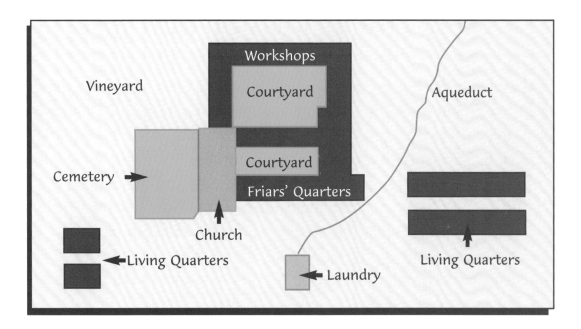

The quadrangle was finished in 1827. Among the buildings constructed were a guardhouse, a guest house, and a *monjerío,* or a women's dormitory. A soap factory and tannery were also included in the quadrangle.

An aqueduct, or water system, stood behind the quadrangle. In the front of the mission was a fountain, complete with a *lavandería.* The *lavandería* was a huge basin used for washing clothes and bathing.

As you study Mission San José, you may find some sources that call it Mission San José de Guadalupe. In the early 1900s, a sign was built and hung from the museum roof that said:

MISSION SAN JOSÉ DE GUADALUPE

All the original record books, however, refer to the mission as it was named at its founding: Mission San José.

Daily Life at Mission San José

Life at the San José mission, as well as at the other missions, varied little from day to day. The schedule was set by the ringing of the bells. Every mission had at least two bells. One bell rang when it was time to pray, and the other bell rang for work, mealtimes, and rest.

A typical day began shortly after sunrise, when all the mission occupants went to the mission church to pray. An hour later, the bell rang for breakfast. Usually the meal was a large bowl of *atole*, a porridge made from corn. By 7:00 A.M., the workday began. The first break was at noon, when the neophytes and missionaries ate lunch, then took a nap, called a *siesta*.

Everyone went back to work around 2:00 P.M. Three hours later, the missionaries held prayers and devotions, short lessons and readings from the Bible. At 6:00 P.M., the dinner bell rang, and the rest of the evening was free time. Free time consisted of dancing, games, or relaxation. The nighttime bell signaling bedtime rang at 8:00 P.M. for the women and at 9:00 P.M. for the men.

It was the friars' responsibility to educate the neophytes in their new religion. They taught them prayers and songs to worship God. The missionaries also led the young children in studies each morning and afternoon while the adults worked.

While the missionaries never gained financially from the Indians' work, they had to make sure the neophytes learned a trade so the mission could make money. This meant they were sometimes forced to discipline those neophytes who did not do their jobs or who tried to

The ringing of the bells governed daily life at the mission. The bells rang when it was time to wake up, ▶ *work, sleep, eat, pray, and play.*

Diego Rivera's mural of the Spanish conquest shows how some Spanish abused the Indians of New Spain.

escape to their villages. The missionaries had the soldiers help in this area. The soldiers were responsible for finding the neophytes who ran away. They were often responsible for punishing the Indians as well.

Those neophytes who worked hard to please the missionaries were free from harm, but those who longed for their old way of life often had to deal with beatings or even being jailed and locked in shackles.

Neophytes labored at a number of tasks to keep the mission running. They learned to weave, farm, tan leather, and make tools.

Gardening and raising cattle were important to the survival of all the missions. Not only was the cattle's meat used for food, but the hides were used to cover bed frames and the seats of chairs. Some hides were turned into buckets or nailed to door frames to make doors. Hides were valuable and the missions traded them for other things that they needed.

Before the Ohlone women came to Mission San José, they and their ancestors had woven baskets from plants and had woven cloth from fur and feathers. The Spanish, however, introduced them to weaving looms, spinning wheels, and materials like cotton and wool, from which the Indian women learned to weave blankets and clothing.

As the years passed, the growth of the mission population slowed. Many neophytes were given the task of recruiting other California

Raising cattle was very important to the survival of those who inhabited the missions. It provided food and leather. The fat from the cattle was made into tallow, which became soap and candles used in the missions.

Cattle raising was the largest moneymaker for the missions. Every mission had its own individual brand that was used to mark its cattle.

Indians into the mission system. They were sent out to their old villages and to other tribes miles away with orders to bring back new neophytes. Often, Indians were brought back against their will.

Fray Buenaventura Fortuni and Fray Narciso Duran

Fray Buenaventura Fortuni and Fray Narciso Duran worked together at Mission San José for 20 years, beginning in 1806. They trained the Ohlone Indians in many trades, from weaving and blacksmith work, to furniture building and shoemaking. The women were taught to wash clothes, sew, and cook.

Fray Duran was known among the missions as a naturally gifted musician. He passed

Music was an important part of life for both the Indians and the friars. This is sheet music written by Fray Duran, a gifted musician.

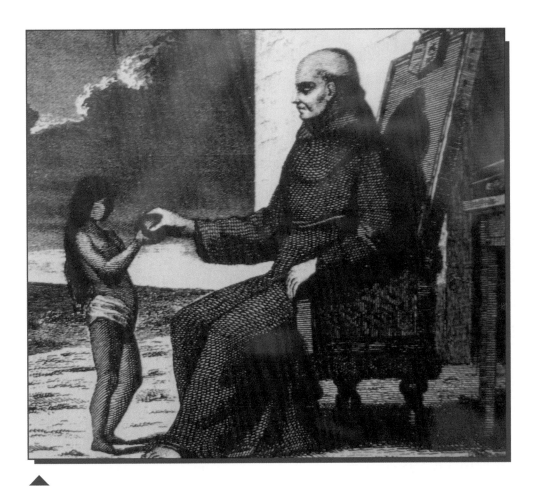

This picture shows Fray Duran with a young California Indian.

his enthusiasm on to the Indians, putting together a church choir and an orchestra, and practicing in the inner court of the quadrangle. He taught the Ohlone to read music, sing harmony, and play instruments. At first the Indians creatively built their own musical instruments, but New Spain later supplied them with violins, flutes, and other instruments.

In 1842, long after the mission had been abandoned, a room full of musical instruments was uncovered, including 20 violins, 4 bass viols, 1 drum, and 2 triangles!

31

Troubles at the San José Mission

A New Way of Life

Mission life provided each Native American who joined the mission with food, shelter, and protection from traders and other settlers who often had little regard for the lives of the Indians. However, mission life was very different from the life the Indians once knew. When the missionaries first came to them, the California Indians could not foresee that they would lose their freedom, be forced to give up their way of life, and be kept inside the missions against their will.

Although many neophytes tried to run away, others remained willingly at the missions and genuinely enjoyed positive relationships with the friars. The friars truly wanted to protect the Indians and not harm them in any way. However, they did not understand that the Indians deserved to live the way they always had. The friars

▲ The California Indians had many customs of their own before they joined the missions. Some Indians didn't like not being able to practice their native beliefs.

◀ When the California Indians felt they were mistreated by the soldiers they showed their anger by revolting.

33

did not understand that the Indians' culture was just as important and valuable as their own.

The Revolt at San José

The San José mission was the setting for one of the most famous mission revolts. A respected and popular neophyte who had grown up under the mission system led the revolt. His name was Estanislao.

In 1828, Fray Duran, who was running the mission at the time, gave Estanislao permission to visit his people, who lived inland from the coast, along the Stanislaus River. Instead of returning to the mission, Estanislao sent word to the mission that he would not be coming back. He was tired of mission life and the structure that was forced upon him. He gathered forces of nonmission Indians, some neophytes from the San José mission and some from other northern California missions. The group camped east of San Francisco Bay and had plans to attack and overtake the missions. For several months the group prepared for battle. During this time, Estanislao and his companions also led attacks against innocent settlers who knew nothing of mission life.

While Estanislao and his group were battling, mission soldiers and neophytes who believed in the mission system rallied together to try to stop Estanislao. In 1829, approximately 100 troops gathered to fight Estanislao and his men.

A battle between the two groups left many of Estanislao's warriors dead. Estanislao went back to the San José mission. Many soldiers and others wanted this traitor killed for his rebellion. Instead, Fray Duran got the governor to pardon him, and he lived there for several more years, until he died from smallpox.

Before the revolt, mission life was usually orderly with routines for work, prayer, and study.

Disease and Population Decline

The biggest problem at Mission San José, and at every other California mission, was the threat of disease for the California Indians. When the Spanish came over from Europe, they brought with them illnesses, such as measles, smallpox, pneumonia, and mumps. The Indians had never been exposed to these diseases. Their immune systems were not equipped to fight them and thousands died. In fact, because of these diseases, the California Indian population was drastically reduced during this time in history.

In 1805, Spanish soldiers unknowingly brought measles and smallpox to Mission San José. By 1810, the San José mission population had dropped from 800 to 545. Hundreds of California Indians had died and many others had fled, afraid for their lives.

The mission cemetery was the final resting place for both the Spanish ▶ and Indians.

◀ *Lack of immunity to European diseases caused many Indians to become sick and die.*

37

The Secularization of the Missions

As Mission San José entered the 1820s, it had one of the strongest economies of all the missions. It was self-sufficient, producing enough goods to trade with the outside world and growing the food necessary to satisfy all its inhabitants.

In 1821, Spain lost the Mexican War of Independence, and Alta California became part of Mexico. This had a destructive effect on the California mission system.

In 1834, the Mexican government passed a law called the Act of Secularization. Secularization meant taking financial control of the missions away from the Catholic Church. The missions would be taken away from the Franciscan friars. This meant that the missions would no longer be used to convert California Indians to Christianity, and the Indians would be free to leave.

Although the missionaries' original intent was to create a self-sufficient culture for the Indians on the mission grounds, they felt the neophytes were not yet ready to be on their own. The Indians themselves had mixed feelings. Some were eager to leave the structured setting, while others were at a loss for what their future would hold without the support of the missions. Secularization forced them to make a change.

Some Indians returned to their villages or went to work at ranches where they were often mistreated and underpaid. Other Indians remained at the secularized mission because they had nowhere else to go. Many of their villages no longer existed. They could no longer hunt

The mission compound was very large and included the church, friars quarters, workshops, Indian ▶ housing, vineyards, and orchards.

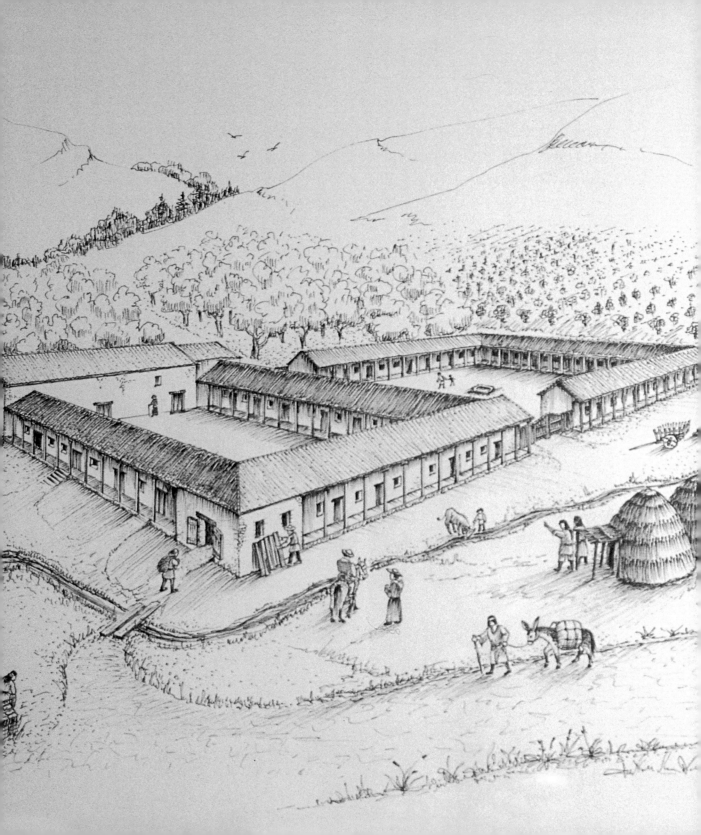

because the mission cattle and sheep had driven off much of the wild game. The wild trees and bushes had been eaten by the livestock or cut down and made into furniture. Their language and ceremonial rituals were forgotten. Without their own culture, many California Indians did not have the means to live better lives in freedom than they did at the missions.

Mexico's original intention of secularization was to turn the mission lands over to the Indians, but this did not happen. In April 1832, José Figueroa was appointed governor of the California territory. Two years later, Governor Figueroa began to secularize the missions. He never planned to turn the rich lands over to the California Indians, who had made it their home for centuries. Instead he sold the lands for a huge profit, often taking the cattle and other mission assets.

San José was secularized in 1836, and its Ohlone population dwindled. Many of the mission's buildings were vandalized and robbed of their assets. In 1848, the mission became a general store and hotel to accommodate the rush of gold seekers. Under the leadership of U.S. president Millard Fillmore, California became the 31st state in 1850. Three years later, the mission became a town church called Saint Joseph's. It stood until the violent earthquake of 1868.

▲
California became a state when Millard Fillmore was president of the United States.

This is an early photo of Mission San José in 1852.

Mission San José Today

If you visit Mission San José today, you may be surprised at how new it looks with its white adobe walls and deep-red tile roof. Mission San José underwent a complete reconstruction in the early 1980s, including the building of an authentic mission church on the foundation of the original adobe church.

Mission San José was reconstructed in the 1980s.

The first permanent church structure, finished in 1809, was destroyed by the 1868 earthquake. It was immediately replaced by a wooden, Gothic-style church, which was built right on top of the old church's foundation. Plans to duplicate the original Ohlone-built church began in 1973. In 1982, the wooden church was moved to another site, so that the restructuring of the authentic-looking adobe mission church could begin.

Three years later, the reconstructed Mission San José was complete. The groups supporting the restoration, the Committee for the Restoration of Mission San José and the Diocese of Oakland, took care that most of the construction was done with

Adobe bricks were used to rebuild the mission.

◀ Visitors come to see the restored Mission San José. It is an important part of California history.

43

More than 150,000 bricks were used to complete the restored San José church.

tools similar to those used by the missionaries and the Ohlone.

Adobe bricks were used in the restoration, but a special mixture was added to keep the bricks from melting as they had on the original structure.

Today the rooms where the missionaries once slept are a part of a small museum. The church continues to hold services in its sanctuary.

The four bells that originally hung in the first adobe church were dispersed to other churches after the earthquake. During the

The gray-robed Franciscan friars lived a simple life at the mission. ▶

This is the main altar in the church at Mission San José.

reconstruction of Mission San José, the four original bells were returned to the mission and hung in the newly restored tower. The bells no longer ring to signal the mission inhabitants to pray or work or sleep or eat, but rather they ring only on special occasions. One can't help but think of the rich story these bells tell through their ringing, of the mixing of two cultures, and the history of the state of California.

Like the other 20 missions built along the California coast, Mission San José played a vital role in the development of California.

This is the bell tower at Mission San José.

A young girl looks at a bell from Mission San José. ▶

A statue of Fray Serra stands in the garden of Mission San José.

The Spanish introduced farming, which is very important to the state's economy. The Spanish also encouraged new cities and towns to be built throughout California. If you live in or visit California, you will notice streets, cities,

Today Mission San José sits on busy Mission Boulevard and is a reminder of a rich piece of California's history.

▲

Many Native Americans and Spanish people gave their lives to build the California missions.

parks, and schools named after important Spanish or American Indian influences. When you see these places, think of the Spanish and Indian people who helped make California what it is today.

This headstone reads: "Here Sleep Four Thousand of the Ohlone Tribe Who Helped the Padres Build This Mission ▶ San José de Guadalupe. Sacred Be Their Memory."

HERE SLEEP
FOUR THOUSAND OF THE
OHLONE TRIBE
WHO HELPED THE PADRES BUILD THIS
MISSION SAN JOSE DE GUADELUPE
SACRED BE THEIR MEMORY

Make Your Own Model Mission San José

To make your own model of Mission San José, you will need:

foamcore   Popsicle sticks
scissors   white and brown paint
cardboard   sand
glue   miniature trees and flowers
tape

Directions

Step 1: Cut a 21" x 10" (53.3 x 25.4 cm) piece of foamcore to use as a base.

10" (25.4 cm)

21" (53.3 cm)

Adult supervision is suggested.

Step 2: To make the side walls of the church, cut four 6″ by 8″ (15.2 x 20.3 cm) pieces of cardboard.

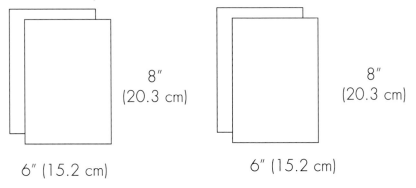

8″
(20.3 cm)

8″
(20.3 cm)

6″ (15.2 cm)

6″ (15.2 cm)

Step 3: Choose one of these pieces for the front wall of the church. Cut a door and two small windows into the front wall.

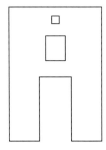

Step 4: Glue the front, back, and side walls of the church together. Tape the inside corners. Attach the church building to the base.

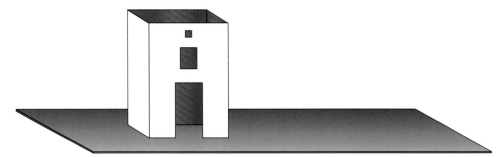

Step 5: Cut two cardboard shapes for the support walls added to the side of the church. One should be 6" (15.2 cm) tall. The other should be 4" (10.2 cm) tall.

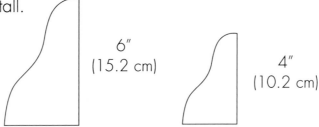

6"
(15.2 cm)

4"
(10.2 cm)

Step 6: Glue the support walls so that they stick out from one of the side walls of the church.

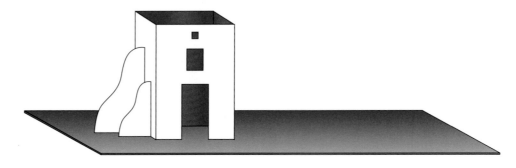

Step 7: Cut an 8.5"x 7.5" (21.5 x 19 cm) piece of cardboard for the church roof. Fold in half, lengthwise, so that the roof will be pointed. Cut an 11.5" by 6" (29.2 x 15.2 cm) piece of cardboard for the roof of the friars' quarters. Fold in half, lengthwise.

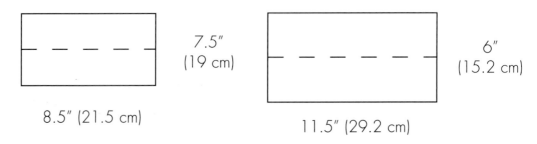

7.5"
(19 cm)

6"
(15.2 cm)

8.5" (21.5 cm)

11.5" (29.2 cm)

54

Step 8: Glue the roof to the church.

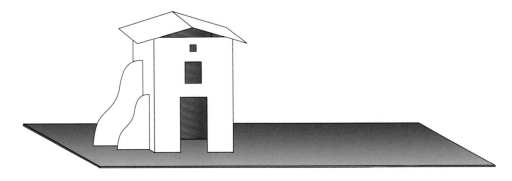

Step 9: For the missionaries' quarters, cut two long walls that measure 11" x 7" (27.9 x 17.8 cm). Cut a third piece for the end wall that measures 4.5" x 7" (11.4 x 17.8 cm).

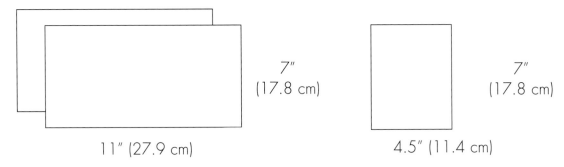

7"
(17.8 cm)

7"
(17.8 cm)

11" (27.9 cm)

4.5" (11.4 cm)

Step 10: Cut four small, square windows into one of the long walls.

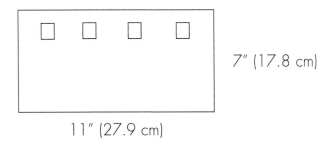

7" (17.8 cm)

11" (27.9 cm)

Step 11: Cut a door into the small end wall. Cut a window above the door.

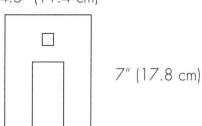

4.5" (11.4 cm)

7" (17.8 cm)

Step 12: Glue together the three walls of the missionaries' quarters and attach them to the side of the church that does not have support walls.

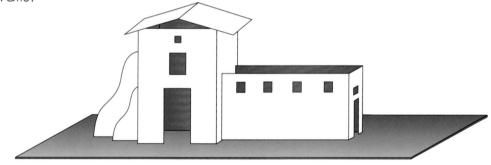

Step 13: Paint two Popsicle sticks brown. Break the sticks into pieces and glue them along the top edge of each of the windows and doors.

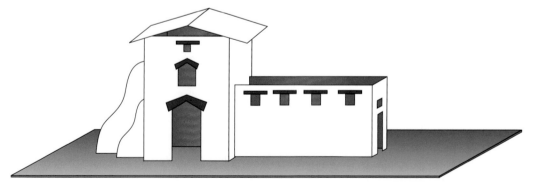

Step 14: Mix sand with white paint. Paint the mission walls with this mixture.

Step 15: Glue the friar's quarters roof onto the building. Paint the roofs brown.

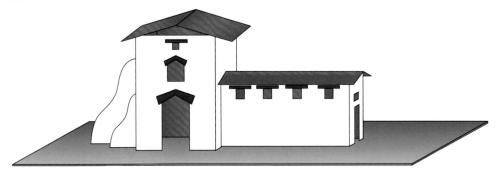

Step 16: Decorate the mission grounds with trees, rocks, and flowers.

*Use the above mission as a reference for building your mission.

Important Dates in Mission History

1492	Christopher Columbus reaches the West Indies
1542	Cabrillo's expedition to California
1602	Sebastián Vizcaíno sails to California
1713	Fray Junípero Serra is born
1769	Founding of San Diego de Alcalá
1770	Founding of San Carlos Borromeo de Carmelo
1771	Founding of San Antonio de Padua and San Gabriel Arcángel
1772	Founding of San Luis Obispo de Tolosa
1776	Founding of San Juan Capistrano
1776	Founding of San Francisco de Asís
1776	Declaration of Independence is signed
1777	Founding of Santa Clara de Asís
1782	Founding of San Buenaventura
1784	Fray Serra dies
1786	Founding of Santa Bárbara
1787	Founding of La Purísima Concepción
1791	Founding of Santa Cruz and Nuestra Señora de la Soledad
1797	**Founding of San José**, San Juan Bautista, San Miguel Arcángel, and San Fernando Rey de España
1798	Founding of San Luis Rey de Francia
1804	Founding of Santa Inés
1817	Founding of San Rafael Arcángel
1823	Founding of San Francisco Solano
1848	Gold found in northern California
1850	California becomes the 31st state

Glossary

adobe (uh-DOH-bee) Sun-dried bricks made of straw, mud, and sometimes manure.

Alta California (AL-tuh ka-luh-FOR-nyuh) The area where the Spanish settled missions, today known as the state of California.

convert (kon-VERT) To cause someone to change beliefs or religions.

depict (dee-PIKT) To represent by drawing, painting, or describing.

Franciscan (fran-SIS-kin) A member of a Catholic religious group started by Saint Francis of Assisi in 1209.

friar (FRY-ur) A brother in a communal religious order. Friars can also be priests.

missionary (MIH-shuh-nayr-ee) A person who teaches his or her religion to people who have different beliefs.

neophyte (NEE-uh-fyt) An American Indian who has converted to another religion.

quadrangle (KWAH-drayn-gul) The square at the center of a mission that is surrounded by four buildings.

revolt (ree-VOLT) To turn away from and fight against a leader.

sanctuary (SANK-choo-wehr–ee) A sacred place, such as church.

secularization (seh-kyoo-luh-rih-ZAY-shun) A process by which the mission lands were made to be nonreligious.

self-sufficient (SELF-suh-FIH-shent) Able to provide for one's own needs without outside aid.

shaman (SHAH-min) A medicine man who is thought to use magic to heal the sick and control other events in people's lives.

tule (TOO-lee) Reeds used by Indians to make houses and boats.

viceroy (VYS-roy) A governor who rules and acts as the representative of the king.

Pronunciation Guide

atole (ah-TOH-lay)

El Camino Real (EL kah-MEE-noh RAY-al)

fray (FRAY)

lavandería (lah-bahn-deh-REE-ah)

monjerío (mohn-hay–REE-oh)

rancherías (rahn-cheh-REE-ahs)

siesta (see-EHS-tah)

Resources

To learn more about the California missions, check out these books, videos, and Web sites:

Books

Time-Life Books. *The Spanish West*. Alexandria, VA: Time-Life Books, 1979.

Emanuels, George. *California Indians, an Illustrated Guide*. Walnut Creek, CA: Diablo Books, 1990.

Hogan, Elizabeth. *The California Missions*. Menlo Park, CA: Sunset Publishing, 1991.

Webb, Edith Buckland. *Indian Life at the Old Missions*. Lincoln, NE and London: University of Nebraska Press, 1982.

Videos

Missions of California: Father Junípero Serra.
Produced by Chip Taylor Productions.
This 11-minute, full-color video features pictures of Father Serra, detailed maps, and beautiful scenery from many of the missions he founded. This should be available at your library.

Web Sites

Due to the changing nature of Internet links, PowerKids Press has developed an online list of Web sites related to the subject of this book. This site is updated regularly. Please use this link to access the list: www.powerkidslinks.com/moca/sjdgu/

Index